The
Greystone
Surveillance

By

Publius

The Greystone Surveillance

Printed in the United States
By Piscataqua Press
www.piscataquapress.com

ISBN: 9781944393915

Dedication:

To all who will compromise
for the greater good.

Day One
March 24, 2018

Boston, MA 3:23 PM
Hi Slops. RU OK? Beginning to worry.

Front Royal, VA 5:30 PM
Sure Johnny, Sorry I haven't answered your emails. Been pretty busy – funny new assignment. I am fine. Talk later.

Boston, MA 6:00 PM
Running the dining hall at good old Greystone Lodge again?

Front Royal 6:05 PM
Nope. Reception had a strange group check in. They took the whole wing and the fireplace lounge. Sealed it all off right away. Margaret was going to do serve them but she got sick. They put me in at the last minute. The boss said I'm supposed to do nothing except cater to their needs 24/7. I'm even sleeping here, too. There are three men and three women, all in their thirties I would say and one older guy in his sixties they called Reverend. When they checked in, Will the porter thought he saw one of the guys had a pistol

1

under his coat. I haven't seen any guns in the fireplace lounge, but it creeps me out. They're not even going to the dining room for their meals, I have to take their orders and bring it to the fireplace lounge. They may not go anywhere except perhaps a walk in the woods trail around the pond.

It's weird, Johnny. I'm supposed to leave them alone when not actually serving them, but I can hang out in the waiter's pantry and hear everything they say. When they first came together I overheard the older guy, the Reverend Robert, say, "Look everybody, we all know why we are here and what we are going to at least try to do. As terribly important as it is, we also know that it is going to be hard and at times, probably, unpleasant. My part is to facilitate, to help you do it." Johnny, he also told them he had helped lots of other groups, some here at Greystone.

He ended by cautioning them. "Look, I know I can help you succeed and make your principals happy. I need you to follow my suggestions beginning with this one: for the next twenty-four hours do not mention, let alone discuss, the issue or the work which brings us here. The most important thing now is for us to become closer to one another; if we do this, the discussions and disputes that will come will be less likely to frustrate our entire effort." He put his finger to his lips and asked. "Can we agree to say not a single word until this time tomorrow?"

Boston, MA 6:10 PM
What do you think?

Front Royal, VA 6:12 PM
No idea. No one knows anyone else here. They're all strangers but a couple of them, a big fellow, Jack, and a black woman, Mary, lit up like candles when they were introduced in the lounge.

Boston, MA 6:13 PM
Some sort of sex thing? Three girls, three boys away in the woods?

Front Royal, VA 6:14 PM
Maybe, or the mafia. At least one maybe has a gun.

Boston, MA 6:14 PM
What's happening now?

Front Royal, VA 6:20 PM
They're taking a break before dinner at 7:00 PM. All afternoon, the old guy had them doing weird things like interviewing and then introducing each other to the group. They're from all over and they had to tell each other about their home states – California, Texas, Montana – nobody from Virginia or Massachusetts, but somebody is from Connecticut. They even had to sing a song to each other. It got pretty silly and there was a lot of laughter. The Reverend had me bring in wine and

beer at 5:00 PM and several of them drank a little too much. I think it was because they knew that whatever it is they are going to do, it wasn't going to happen until tomorrow at 2:15 PM, so they were all free as could be. Jack and Mary have definitely got something going already. There's going to be dinner and some film the Reverend has set up, then bed time. They're coming back down tomorrow for breakfast. I already have their orders.

Boston, MA 6:21PM
This is cool, Slops. I want you to keep a very close eye on this and tell me everything. There might be a story here.

Front Royal, VA 6:21 PM
Promise to stop calling me Slops? After all, we're not children any more.

Boston, MA 6:22 PM
I know, Sis. It's just a habit. What can I say? Older siblings suck. Maybe I'll stop someday.

Front Royal, VA 6:22 PM
If this turns out to mean something, will your employer send me a big check?

Boston, MA 6:25 PM
Maybe. *The Boston Globe* can be pretty generous sometimes.

Front Royal, VA 6:25PM
OK Big Brother. Till tomorrow.

Boston, MA 6:25 PM
BTW, Have you decided yet?

Front Royal, VA 6:26PM
About next year?

Boston, MA 6:26 PM
Of course! You're more than half way through your gap year already. They won't extend the admission at BU forever, even for a smarty-pants like you.

Front Royal, VA 6:26PM
I know, I know.

Boston, MA 6:26 PM
OK, AA. Looking forward to the morning report. What the hell is this all about?

Day Two
March 25, 2018

Front Royal, VA 10:15 AM

Morning Bro, I'll do my best to report what happened. Last night they frolicked about until 10:30 PM or so, and then they all went to their rooms. Whatever they are here for, they still haven't said… just like the Reverend told them, a forbidden topic. I get the feeling it is like a lull before a storm here; they just want to enjoy it while they can, for whatever is coming is going to be real bad. Anyway, this morning, the Reverend has brought in a truckload of plastic pipes and fittings along with some tools, and instructed them to "Create something. The something is something, true, but the something I hope for is your experience, your successful experience for the six of you working together and achieving a solid goal. And have fun at the same time, please. And a caution; it is not 2:15 PM yet, no? So some things are still off limits, yes?"

They're deep into it now. Kind of funny to watch. I have learned this much; they all are from the DC area and I think they are all connected to the government somehow. I've overheard references to places in DC and "markups" and stuff like that. Hearings, too.

Boston, MA 10:25 AM
Now you're getting somewhere Sis. Relieved it isn't the mafia. Can U tape it?

Front Royal, VA 10:25 AM
Come on, Johnny. That would be illegal, wouldn't it? You want me to go to jail? Besides, I doubt I could pull it off without getting caught.

Boston, MA 10:25 AM
OK, OK. Give me an update this afternoon. I've got to run. As much detail as you can.

Front Royal, VA 10:25 AM
Funny thing, Johnny. They've pretty much forgotten I am there at all. Just part of the woodwork now. Almost one of them. Just having fun.

Boston, MA 10:26 AM
Cool. Bye.

Front Royal, VA 1:30 PM
Johnny. Holy Cow. They're all big shots from the Capitol. And I think we may have a real problem here, Johnny. I'll tell you. At lunch, the old guy, the Reverend started talking and held sway for the whole meal. He handed out a roster of the attendees. I'll send a picture here.

Greystone Lodge
March 24, 2018 - TBD

Joyce Benoit – room 9
Mason (D)
California 857 396-1137

Doreen Dodge – room 5
Colebrook (R)
Vermont 588 794-4921

Harlan Drake- room 7
Tyler (R)
Texas 519 903-5793

Mary Kidd – room 4
Porcello (D)
New York 774 388-2856

Jack Robinson – room 8
Ward (R)
Montana 548 322-1864

Michael Rovaldi – room 6
Alston (D)
Connecticut 771 499-3783

Reverend Robert Mansfield
137 Depot Road
Front Royal, VA 22630
477 922-6404

They are all aides to US Senators, Johnny. Can U believe that?!! Something big is happening. The Reverend praised each of them. Said he was impressed with what great choices the senators had made. Observing the aides working together, he said, convinced him that if anyone could handle the work ahead, they could. Then he talked about the qualities he had observed in each one. Jack Robinson is a decorated Marine veteran from Afghanistan and is chief of staff for Senator Ward of Montana. Joyce Benoit is a senior member of Senator Mason's staff in California. She was an ACLU attorney previously. Every one of them exhibited what the Reverend called, "affinity for the common cause." He said it was an essential quality: a successful joint outcome was the primary goal. The others, Harlan, Michael, Mary and Doreen are relatively new to the Washington scene. Most of them are married or partnered up in some way, a few have kids even, but the Jack and Mary pair it appears are not. Reverend Mansfield told how the group came together. He said, two very senior Senators, Tyler and Alston were in the Senate Gym talking shop. He reported that as Tyler recalled it the conversation went:

Tyler: We can't move anything because our constituents are so adamant, so unwilling to compromise at all.

Ward: Not to mention our major funders. We both know who they are, and they all always champion the most extreme positions.

9

Tyler: Then again, we may just be too old. You know, forgotten how to do it any other way. Pure habit now; nothing will ever change (and we know it) so we just pretend to try- not really expecting any progress at all.

Ward: True, true. And we just end up accusing each other of being unreasonable. Don't you hate it sometimes?

Tyler: I do, I do indeed. This endless recrimination and wheel spinning. All the people out there who are pissed off at us for getting nowhere. Well, what the hell, Ben. Why don't we turn it over to the kids on our staffs and see if they can do any better. Get a representative, balanced group from both sides together far away from the public eye and see if they can come up with a solution.

Ward: If we can keep it secret, there doesn't seem to be anything to lose, I guess.

Tyler: Let's talk to a few on each side quietly and see where it leads. There's a recess coming up in March. That would be a good time to do it if it can be done at all.

Reverend Mansfield said he was contacted by an old friend and colleague, Senator Smith of Virginia. Would he, Mansfield, be willing to plan and facilitate such an effort as he had so many others? Somewhere near the DC area but not too near, staying out of sight would be critical. "Of course," the Reverend replied, "I would love to, and even if I did not, given the polarized and paralyzed state of the nation today, it is my patriotic duty to help in any way I can. I am completely unbiased and I have facilitated groups a hundred times, so yes, I will do it." The plan was to meet here at the Greystone Lodge, about an hour's ride from Washington DC, quite secluded. We can be quite isolated here from the rest of the facility. I believe all of you were kept in the dark until the very last minute? Yes?" Joyce Benoit answered "Yes, but nearly everyone was told they would be needed in Washington over the recess. No one was told why, however, and again, every effort was made to keep it under the radar." Jack Robinson added, "And we've all been told that there is no ending date set here. We have the lodge for the full two weeks if necessary, but we can go home as soon as we finish. Kind of an incentive to really do it this time, eh?"

Johnny, 2:15 PM looms. They're going to start work soon on whatever it is they are here to do, but you can tell, it is super secret. I bet if Margaret hadn't got sick and I hadn't been thrown last minute into the breach here, you wouldn't have heard about this meeting at all. They're trying to keep it all very quiet. Perhaps we should stop?

Boston, MA 1:45 PM
ABSOLUTELY NOT!!!! *You* have not been ordered to keep anything *you* see or hear secret, not one thing. Plus if it is official government work, the country, the people, have a right to know what

they are doing. The room and every one in the room up there is being paid with our tax dollars, and now, even you are, too, so Sister of mine, you damn well keep taking notes and feeding it all to me. Just as much as you can. I'm serious. It is your patriotic duty. You hear?

Front Royal, VA 1:46 PM
OK, they're on break now, lunch over, coming back at 2:15. Gotta go. Alice

Front Royal, VA 4:30 PM
Guns, Johnny. It's all about guns. They're here to try to negotiate a comprehensive solution to the gun controversy. Reverend Mansfield convened them in the Fireside Lounge, they had to move the "creation," a modern sculpture adorned with red, white, and blue bunting the women made me scrounge from the Greystone's supplies, to one side and then move the furniture around. That sculpture is quite something, I tell you, it would win a prize or my name is not Alice Ames. Anyway, they set to work at precisely 2:15 PM, the Reverend Mansfield read a letter jointly signed by each of their bosses; all six Senators. Here is a photo I just snapped while they were taking a break:

To: Joyce Benoit, Doreen Dodge, Harlan Drake Mary Kidd, Jack Robinson, Michael Rovaldi

For decades our nation has been stymied by the conflict between those among us, sincere and patriotic Americans every one, who seek more restrictions and controls over fire arms, and those who seek fewer. If the focus is on the deaths of innocents, the call is for greater restrictions; if the focus is on self defense and individual civil rights, the call is for fewer. Positions range from advocacy of complete restriction, the banning of all guns to positions advocating no restrictions whatever.

The second amendment and current case law (Heller, McDonald, etc) suggests that neither extreme is tenable. We need to describe a reasonable, middle ground that can be tolerated, if not warmly embraced, by all for the long term future. In other words, we yearn for an agreement that both sides can sincerely support.

If ever there was a moment for inspired staff work in this august body, it is now. We charge you with the task of discovering and describing such an agreement. Each of you represents the best America has to offer, you are very well-informed, and we have every confidence that, with the aid of Reverend Mansfield, you will succeed.

God Speed,

Signatories: Senators Alston (Connecticut), Colebrook (Vermont), Mason (California), Porcello (New York), Tyler (Texas), Ward (Montana)

Reverend Mansfield has been sharing data on gun deaths in the country. He had collected a ton of data and presented it all in tables and slides. I don't think the six staff people here can ask a single question about guns, deaths, or mass shootings that Mansfield cannot answer. He even had the latest count of dead in last week's event in Idaho, the one in the soccer stadium. So, it is clear to them all what they have to do, and they have the facts to work with. Heck, they're coming back now. I've got to quit. Alice

Front Royal, VA 5:30 PM

Well blow me down. That was surprising. When they came back at 5:00 PM, they staged a rebellion of sorts. You'd have thought it was funny, Johnny, but they've already become a tight-knit group and they asked, told really, the Reverend that they preferred to take the night off. They would start the work the next morning. The big guy from Montana and the lady from California, they're both a little older I think, they've emerged as sort of leaders. They said everyone was tired, they needed time to process all the data he had flung at them, had to digest the handouts, and so on and on. But you know, Johnny, I think they're just having fun with each other now and don't want to actually start the work just yet. So, the Reverend had little to say about it, and off they all went to get ready for dinner. They will get to the task tomorrow morning.

Boston, MA 6:00 PM

OK Slops, oops Sorry. I promised not to call you that. Sister Alice. You are doing great. Keep it up. Filch a copy of every hand out if you can and overnight them to me as soon as you get the chance. Go Girl.

Day Three
March 26, 2018

Front Royal, VA 7:30 AM

Morning Brother. Last night was a party. It started just as they gathered for drinks and dinner. They did talk a little about guns. It was all tentative probing not about their general positions, they all could guess given the party affiliations of their bosses, but about intensity; how zealously each was wed to the party lines. But mostly they avoided the topic and simply wanted to talk about everything else, prolonging the moment when they would have to start. After dinner, they played an impromptu game of charades and they all were really silly again. Later, they all put on their jackets and went out for another walk around the lake. I can't say for sure Johnny, but it really does look like Mary from New York is falling head over heels for the big guy, Jack, from Montana. They were still out there somewhere after everyone else, including me, were in bed. Nine is the start time. The Reverend isn't here yet.

Front Royal, VA 10:40 AM

Wow, Johnny. What a morning! The Reverend arrived in time for breakfast and really cracked the whip. He said the Senators, their bosses, all were counting on them and had high hopes. He also appealed to their patriotism. He pointed out that a lot depended on them to deliver: the peace and unity of the nation and probably a great many American lives. He asked, "Does anyone here think there are too few deaths by guns in America?" and of course no one raised a hand. Then he asked, "Are the numbers of deaths just right?" Again, no one raised a hand. So he concluded, "We at least can start with agreement on that point; there are too many." Then they went through the data sheets he had provided and confirmed the number of deaths by murder, suicide, mass murder, and accident. They also identified the number killed by pistol, rifle, shot gun, and semi-automatic rifle. In each step, they agreed with the number as a fact. The Reverend was suggesting they brainstorm ways to reduce the numbers in each category, when Harlan Drake, the Texan, drawled, "Remember the law. We have one you know. Remember the Bill of Rights? No screwing around with my right to free speech, free peaceable assembly, free press, free religion, and free right to keep and bear arms. The Supreme Court in the Heller and MacDonald decisions makes it clear; we have a right to guns." He was a little truculent I thought.

Well, that sort of derailed the Reverend's plan for awhile. Michael Rovaldi from Connecticut reacted first. "Well, that is true, Harlan, but there are no *absolute* civil rights are there? Even speech. It is free but up to the point that your speech injures someone else, say like hollering fire in a crowded theater. So, it is possible to restrict gun ownership. We already do. No machine guns, you know. No bazookas or artillery cannons in your neighbor's back yard. We even banned AR 15 type rifles from 1994 to 2004."

Joyce Benoit, added, "Those are army type weapons, right? They belong locked up in armories."

"Not at all," Harlan replied. "The militiamen owned their own rifles and pistols and kept them at home. In part they followed the Swiss model"

"Just because they were in the militia, right? The second amendment is all about maintaining the militia. What is it," Michael quoted, "A well-regulated militia being necessary to the maintenance and security of a free state, the right of the people to keep and bear arms shall not be infringed. Hell, man. It is all one sentence uttered in one breath. Militia and guns."

The Reverend responded. "Well, Michael, not exactly all and only about the militia. As we know, and Harlan just pointed out, the Supreme Court analyzed the thinking of the founders who signed off on the Constitution and the Bill of Rights. They concluded that individual citizens, whether in militia's or not, have the right to own and carry arms around. In fact, the right preempts even the Constitution; it is based on English law and the concept that individuals have the right to defend themselves if attacked."

"But the founders never ever would have condoned it had they known how lethal today's weapons can be. We are talking 18th Century versus 21st Century." Michael objected.

Again, the Reverend gently disagreed. "We can't know what they would say now. It is clear, reading their words at the time, that the moment Washington, Jefferson, Adams, Madison, Henry, and a bunch more were brought back to life today, they would ask, 'what is the standard arm of the average soldier?' and they would say, 'that is the arm each American white male from the age of 18 to 56 should buy himself and keep in his house along with a basic load of ammunition for his personal defense and if called upon, for the defense of the state and country. They would see US Soldiers carrying M16 rifles and say, every male in the age range should own and keep one at home along with five magazines of ammunition, too. There can be no doubt about that given what is recorded in the old archives." The Reverend then smiled, and continued, "But we all know they were the brightest and most reasonable men of their age, no fools certainly, and how they would react when the saw what an M16, or an AR15, with their 20 – 30 round detachable magazines can do, especially against unarmed school children, massed concert goers, and throngs attending theaters or clubs is open to conjecture."

"And, there are no militias anymore. What would Washington, Adams, Jefferson, Patrick Henry think about that?" The Californian added that.

Jack from Montana jumped in noting, "Actually, there was a law from 1792 to 1903, the Militia Act and every male was expected to buy and keep his own long gun at home. They amended the law after the Civil War to require all the black men to do the same."

"Why did the repeal it in 1903?" The Vermonter, Doreen Dodge's question.

Harlan's answer, "Because they activated the National Guard. It took the place of the militias. The guards report to the state's governors, just as the militias did before them, unless they are federalized. You know, like they did in the fifties to desegregate the Alabama schools."

Mary from New York. "Then if there are no longer militias, why have all these Army type guns all over the streets?"

That question got them going and the arguments began to get heated. That's when Mansfield called a half hour break. He again told them to stand back from it all and talk about other things for awhile and come back at 11:00AM. They've taken their coffees and sodas out on the patio. Alice

Front Royal, VA 4:35 PM
Johnny, when they got back from break this

20

morning, Doreen Dodge from Vermont asked if anyone knew what kind of weapon the soldiers carried when the militias were abandoned in 1903 in favor of the National Guard. Harlan Drake from Texas knew the answer; the 1903 Springfield rifle. It was a bolt action rifle with a four round magazine. Doreen asked what bolt action meant, and Harlan gave everyone a review of the different ways of getting a spent cartridge out of the rifle and a new one loaded and ready to fire. Bolt actions, lever actions were the two common ways until semi automatic and fully automatic machine guns were invented for WWI.

"So it was WWI that created the mess we're in now?" Doreen's question. Mary chimed in. "Guns, guns. Too many, and too lethal? What should we do?"

"Limit the hell out of them, I say," Joyce of California. "We're getting these mass shootings every week, almost every day, now. You are right on, Mary. Too many, too lethal."

Harlan said, "Well, that's just not true. But you do realize, don't you, there are millions and millions of guns in the US, and they do no harm. There probably are eight to twelve million AR 15 style sporting rifles out there in civilian hands now – too many to ever buy back anyway. It would cost billions. Look, no gun in the rack, or propped behind the front door, ever killed anybody. It's only when somebody picks it up and uses it does it do any harm at all. Let's not blame the guns. It's the mentally ill fools who pick them up and go off the reservation. Blame them. Then he really shocked them all. He took out a pistol he had under his shirt and laid it on the table. There were gasps, but he said, "It is a SIG Sauer p320. It is unloaded and harmless. All the rounds are locked in the safe in my room. This is just a pile of metal parts, but a pile with tremendous potential. He grinned. Come on, pass it around everyone. Stop demonizing guns. Look, I believe everyone here is a patriotic, sane, American, and it is our right to own guns, period. I certainly agree that we are having too many of these mass shootings in schools, but hey look, there were 30 million kids attending school during the last one in Florida. Only a dozen were killed and what was it, maybe thirty wounded."

Mary Kidd from New York jumped to her feet. "I can't believe this. Because 30 million kids were not killed, we should be sanguine about senselessly, needlessly killing twelve? Come on, Harlan, you can't be serious. It's an infection, each time, tearing at the heart of our republic. We either become calloused or fearful. I'm telling you, it is personal for me; my niece, Shana was killed, one of the ten, in the 2013 Altoona shooting. Aunt Rose and Uncle Jamal never recovered. There were 1,624 mass shooting in the past 1,870 days. It is ruining our culture. It is just unacceptable, this sick, sick, status quo." She sat down. I thought she was going to cry. There was a long silence, and Jack Robinson spoke first, "Well, Mary, I can see now why Governor Procello picked you to be here. You're authentic all right."

Harlan added. "Mary, I doubt that many have actually occurred, but I am sorry for your family's loss." She hissed, "And I bet you'll send them your thoughts and prayers, too."

The Reverend Mansfield jumped up then told them to take another hike around the lake, "You're voices are all too tense. Please, go and relax. Find that common center again."

They were very subdued when they got back. Doreen Dodge put out the idea that the new surge of mass shootings could have something to do with the development of video games. "You know, they make mowing down dozens and dozens of people look like fun, a game. Kids become used to it all and it isn't shocking, hardly real." Others pointed out that in Europe, Japan, all over, the kids play just as many video games but there aren't mass shootings like here. "That's because they don't have the eight to twelve million assault rifles." Mary from NY. Jack from Montana said, "It may be some of both here; anyone who has been in combat a while has to recognize that the longer you are in it the more adapted, desensitized, you get. It is a coarsening of the soul and it is adaptive; it helps you keep going and maybe live longer. Intuitively, it makes sense, but there also are a zillion other violent images on TV, the movies, and so on as well as video games." "Yeah, it's a cultural thing." Doreen.

When they returned from lunch at 1:30PM, Reverend Mansfield had a graphic up on the screen and they added notes so it ended up looking like this picture.

CRAZY PERSON: Blocked by screening, testing, banning of the guns → **GUN:** Blocked by armed guards, limited controlled access, concealed carry in crowd, armed victims → **Victim**

He said, "Now look, I've listened to the discussions and it seems to me that the biggest issue is the horrific instances of mass shootings with semiautomatic rifles. If it were not for those events so devastating to the families and communities involved and so offensive to our sense of order and security, we would pay as little attention to gun deaths as we do to motor vehicle deaths, unless of course one's own family is involved, even though most people die of pistol shots, both murders and suicides. So, what do you think? Could we agree to treat guns in two categories; the semi automatic long guns and all the rest? At least for now." None of them seemed thrilled with the idea, but in the end they all agreed. Somebody said, "OK, if we take it a little at a time maybe we can get somewhere. So Reverend Mansfield referred them to the chart. "To prevent the mass shootings you need to keep the crazy person from first, accessing the semiautomatic rifle, and second, getting into position to shoot his victims. Theoretically, but perhaps not practically, you could screen everyone and allow those deemed sane, to purchase the semi automatic. You also could, even if you couldn't prevent the crazy person from getting the gun, encourage his friends, family, neighbors, everyone who senses he is losing control and could do harm to get authorities to intervene. Some states are developing so called 'red flag laws' in this regard. Then, failing that, you could harden all the places where people are massed; the schools, concerts, theaters, etc. We could require any organization and local authorities planning to hold an event in which say fifty people are gathered in one place to have a security and defense plan to prevent a mass shooting incident. "Make them all like airports?" Joyce.

"Can't say," Reverend. "The trouble is, I've listened to all your points of view and all of you favor the one approach but reject the other. Possibly a coordinated effort is called for? Yes? That is what I believe your senators were hoping for whether they realized it or not."

There was a considerable discussion after that and I can't begin to capture it all. Then I think it was Jack who suggested, "You know, whatever approach you pick really shifts responsibility; maybe that is why we have the controversy.

Nobody wants to accept any share of the blame. If you go with the block-them-from-getting-guns-at–all approach, then you put the burden on the federal government. They are the only ones who can impose a ban as they did from 1994 to 2004. And the Feds are required to defend the 2nd Amendment." Then Joyce added, "And if you go with the next approach, shielding the victim, you shift the burden to the local authorities, superintendents of schools, local police chiefs, sheriffs, and so on."

Michael of Connecticut. "Hell, it is the culture and we are all in it, aren't we? Everybody is to blame more or less. We all have a part."

"So come on everyone, why can't everybody get involved? It will probably take a coordinated effort won't it? Certainly nothing's working so far is it?" Doreen Dodge from Vermont.

"Yeah, share the misery; share the solution, right?" Michael I think again.

After a pause, Reverend Mansfield observed, "I think you are making good progress team. You know, cooperation is defined as: An act or instance of working or acting together for a common purpose or benefit; joint action.

I think you are right, if we hope to impact this situation, it probably will require everyone to get involved. Truth is, there is plenty of blame to go around and any serious solution will involve everyone."

The Californian, Joyce, made a key

observation. "You know, it is obvious who gets a pass here; the state governments." Others pointed out the irony that originally the states had everything to do with guns; they ran the militias. They talked and talked about this, and came to a consensus that as far as the semiautomatic rifles went, they were militia-type weapons for the most part. It was unusual for them to be used for hunting or home defense; even target shooting was better served with other types of weapons. Even Jack, who had served in Afghanistan had to agree. "I know people try to present them as multi-use recreational weapons, but that truly is a stretch. You can hunt and shoot cans with them if you want to, but everyone knows they primarily developed and designed for the battlefield."

They've taking a break for dinner now. I have to go get the cart. I think they are getting back to it after dinner. Alice

Front Royal. VA 6:45 PM
They got totally derailed during dinner. Someone, the guy from Connecticut, Rovaldi, said the opposition disrespected and devalued humanity by permitting so many guns to "float about the society willy-nilly. We don't care about the innocents, we're killing them off in droves." Harlan fiercely objected. "Granting individuals the right and the means of self-defense is the foremost measure of respect and value. Trust the individual to behave responsibly as a good citizen. It is what

27

the 2nd Amendment is all about. If you can't see that, you really are a jerk." Joyce Benoit of California calmed them down. "Really, Harlan? Name calling? After all we've been through here. We really can't devolve to that and have any hope of getting out of here before spring recess is over. Two full weeks! Can we?" Everyone retreated to their rooms after that. I don't know if they are coming back or not.

Front Royal, VA 10:15 PM

Well, they did come back. Everyone was in place by 7:10 PM but it was really subdued. Perhaps it was the alcohol they had with dinner, but they got talking about philosophy. I guess it started with different view of mankind that Michael and Harlan had put forth at dinner; part of a collective vs standing as an individual. I couldn't follow any of it, Johnny, but I think I am looking forward to college after this gap year is over. Anyway, the names I heard and can remember were Kant, Descartes, Spinoza, Kierkegaard, Heidegger, Bentham, Nozick, Latour and Ihde. There were a slew of others; these people are really smart. But it didn't seem to have anything to do with guns at all. The Reverend left them at 8:30 PM returning to his home in town. As he left he said, "As for me, I'm in the camp of Charles Pierce and William James, good American Pragmatists all. There is little to be gained from the pursuit of ultimate truths or preordained meanings. The worth of a concept can be determined solely by its consequences in the lives of the people. There are few if any sharp distinctions in nature – most everything is a continuum. That which holds open the door to dialogue, discussion, and the pursuit of further truth is good while that which closes the door and tamps down the quest for knowledge is bad. And of course, Reinhold Niebuhr cautions me to be always a humble and realistic Christian. But in any case, dear friends, our work is not done. I'll see you tomorrow at 9:00 AM sharp. I do believe we are getting closer to a resolution here. Good night young people. Be gentle with each other. Don't stay up too late." They all spent the rest of the evening on their cell phones catching up with friends and family…all except the Mary and Jack who went for a stroll. I heard some of them refer to them as "Jarymack" behind their backs. Bye.

Day Four
March 27, 2018

Boston MA 7:47 AM

Little sister, you are the best. Please major in journalism when you get to college next year. My program up here at BU is a great one; Professor McDougal is the best. I can give you a reference. Keep it up.

Front Royal, VA 10:40 AM

It's almost over, Johnny. After breakfast, Joyce Benoit, the lawyer from California addressed the group. She said, "You know, I've been thinking about what we've talked about, especially about responsibility and blame. It really is true; we can't point fingers. There is no one thing to blame. If our focus is on mass shootings then it is often the case that the shooter ends up dead; either he kills himself or the cops kill him. It is not satisfying to any of us least of all the families of the victims. They want a public accounting; justice. Mass shootings can affect any community and town. Practically every time after the slaughter, it is revealed that the authorities, the neighbors, other members of the family, somebody knew the person, who might have been perfectly normal when the gun was

30

purchased, was beginning to slip. To then drift further and further into insanity...and they did nothing about it. A ton of warning signs and all ignored. We are all to blame. We need to change our culture." "I wish we could go back," the Texan, Harlan, added. "You know, to the days when owning a gun meant something." The ex Marine joined in, "Yeah, in the beginning it was evidence of patriotism to own a gun. You were a militiaman by definition." There was a long, long pause, and Doreen Dodge, the Vermonter suggested, "Then why don't we bring back the idea of state militias? It wouldn't be quite the same of course because now we have the National Guard, but couldn't there still be a role for state militias?" Well, I tell you, Johnny, they ran with this idea right up to the break where they are now. They are all on board with the idea that gun ownership could imply a willingness to act patriotically if called upon to help maintain order or repel an invader, and with respect to semiautomatic rifles, the states could and should manage them as potential assets in their state militias. They're going to pick this up when they get back. Alice

Front Royal, VA 2:30 PM

I couldn't report sooner. Really busy here. They've got a list of commitments someone who owns a gun should make. Here it is on the tag board – it was scary, Johnny, the Reverend almost caught me snapping this picture but I slipped the phone under my dish rag just in time. Anyway, here it is:

Modern Militia

Whether armed or not:

1.   Acknowledge responsibility to help maintain order and peace.

2.   Reach out, try to help when someone is slipping into mental illness, and/or involve the authorities in the situation, and follow through (if the authorities do nothing, notify other authorities, other potential sources of help, etc. persist!!

If armed (Pistol, Rifle, Shotgun):

3.   Commit oneself to the defense of the person, home, community, state and country and to serving in the public interest if requested

If armed with a semi automatic rifle:

4. Register the same with the state militia and abide by the directives given to achieve and maintain a well-regulated militia.

At lunch and after, the pro-gun people pushed back saying "So let me get this straight. We turn the

M16, AR 15 style rifles over to the states' jurisdictions? This is a major compromise. What do we get in return?"

Joyce asked, "What do you want?" Answer: "Leave all the other guns alone. No regulation, no registration, no nothing." Several qualified that: "As long as you can assure that it is never compromised, you understand, prohibit registration of anything other than the semiautomatic rifles, keep the Instant Background Check system in place and make it apply to all transfers"

"You mean private sales, gun shows, the internet, too?" Doreen. "You bet," Joyce answered. "Every transfer. Shouldn't everyone want to do whatever they could to assure themselves they were not passing a gun, any gun, on to someone who shouldn't have it? The background check system can at least help a little with that, can't it?"

Jack the Montanan said, "My dad gave me my first gun when I was twelve. Would the background thing apply there?" That lead to a diversion into what age was appropriate for ownership of guns-it took over an hour - and they concluded that Jack Robinson at twelve actually didn't own the gun; his dad did and that Jack was only watching it for his dad. They settled on 18 as the legal age for gun ownership, providing the background check was passed, and yes it would apply to every transfer. "Hell, Jack," Michael of Connecticut added, "It wouldn't be the end of the world if you, and your dad took the gun to the local licensed gun shop and effected the transfer when you turned eighteen. Up until that point the gun still belonged to your dad. He could loan it to you or anyone else he trusted to use it wisely, but he still was responsible. Kind of like not handing your car keys over to someone who is drunk. Right? Before you give the gun over permanently, going through the background check system means you can be somewhat more sure that you are not turning it over to someone who is incompetent, a criminal, or a terrorist."

Jack said, "Some states make it ridiculously expensive." They argued and argued, but finally agreed that it was so important to have this done that background checks should be a service of the federal government. They didn't want people to avoid it for financial reasons.

Harlan again. "Still, feels like I'm still just giving things up and getting nothing in return."

"Other than the background check, nothing applies to the other guns. No regulation at all, except the age thing, right? That's a good thing isn't it?" Doreen Dodge of Vermont. Jack still had doubts.

"How about this," Harlan said, "if we are shifting some of the gun debate to the states, what if we all agree that the laws of the states regarding guns will apply wherever the citizens of that state go? This would mean both open and concealed carry anywhere in the country if the home state permitted that."

"But not, the semiautomatic rifles we've talked about, right?" Joyce.

"Right, those militia-type weapons could cross state lines only with the concurrence of both governors."

"Call it super-reciprocity." Joyce.

Michael, then added. "I tell you, my state will never agree to any of that. If you come to Hartford laden down with weapons, the police would arrest you on sight."

"Not if this is passed," Joyce said. "A Texan or Montanan would have the right to carry his guns anywhere."

"The Capitol, the Court Houses, the White House, the schools, colleges?" Mary.

"Don't be silly. Of course there would be exceptions, but overall, unless there is some compelling reason otherwise, the laws of the citizen's state would prevail." Joyce.

"Well I can't tell you how unlikely it is that my Governor will accept this idea – at least I can't express it in the extreme terms and language he would use. If I did, Reverend Mansfield would make me go walk around the lake again. (They all laughed.) But for now, I can see that we are struggling to find a compromise so let's just go with it." Michael.

After lunch they picked up on Michael's point. Jack observed that they had made a lot of progress, but Michael's point was valid; how would they sell their ideas to their principals? Was there any hope of a compromise? "I'll be honest: my guy is solidly in the camp of the DSA, that's Defenders of the Second Amendment if you didn't already know. (They all laughed again. They all knew) He had his point of view well-established long ago, but the DSA liked it (a lot), and they've funded his campaigns ever since. Truth is: I'm pretty sure they will not accept any roll back on semiautomatics even with the free release of everything else."

Joyce added, "And the same can be said for Senator Mason. He never changes his mind to accommodate a contributor, but the SAGVA (Stop All Gun Violence Association) has backed him for years in California. It will take a lot for them to accept the image of you Texan's, Harlan, packing heat openly through the streets of San Francisco."

"I have also to point out that the blame so far has always pointed to the federal government (they should ban the semiautomatics like they did before, 1994 -2004.) Reverend Mansfield added, "or the local authorities – they should have better constrained the mentally ill person, should have 'hardened' the school or site, and so on. This plan shifts accountability to the state governments."

"Yes," Joyce the lawyer added, "and in most states, they are unlikely to accept the responsibility because to do so opens a cause for action."

"What's that?" Mary of New York. "If the semiautomatic rifle is a weapon of the well-regulated militia and it is used to mow down a classroom of kids, then the militia can be held accountable, that is, the state can be sued for negligence. I don't know how my Governor would react to that development. And of course, we would not know what it really meant until there were some actual cases and judicial rulings."

They were all really down in the dumps when all of this came up, but the Reverend perked them up just before the afternoon break. He said, "You young people have done a great job here. You have struggled and come up with a new approach, a new compromise on the gun issue. This is exactly what your bosses wanted you to do; apply creative, fresh minds to the stale old, endlessly repetitive, intractable problem. That what you have come up with departs from the status quo should be no surprise, and it isn't up to you to implement it; your principals have that task if they like your ideas. In any case, I believe this is a reasonable compromise. Take heart. When you come back, let's put it into a near final form that we can give to the Senators. I'm optimistic we can finish tonight and perhaps we can all go home tomorrow. OK?" So, they all drifted off for awhile, but they're coming back now. Alice

Front Royal, VA 8:30 PM
Jack and Harlan had a question when they

returned at 3:04 PM today. "What happens if the local militia doesn't accept the fellow with the semiautomatic rifle with its detachable magazine? Say he passed the background check, bought his Bushmaster and five magazines of ammunition, and presented himself to the state's authorities. Then when they vetted him, they found reason to doubt his stability. They wouldn't want him in the militia? What then?"

Joyce of California answered. "It would be a due process issue. They would have to make the case that the person and his Bushmaster should not be in the militia and I believe, while they are making the determination, they should confiscate the gun. They also should have a time limit to convince a judge the man should not have the gun. If the state wins, hey would have to compensate the fellow of course. But that is rather the whole point here isn't it? We have to find some way to keep these highly lethal weapons out of the hands of crazy people. Somebody, somewhere has to do it. The Federal and Local Governments lack the means or the motivation to do it, obviously, so why not leave it up to the states? I suspect that after awhile, the word would get out in each state and it would become known what it would take to pass muster. Those who could not pass would either not bother to purchase the AR 15, or would do so and not attempt to register it and that alone would be a felony. It would be a deterrent at least. Maybe states would publish criteria so people could know before they buy whether or not they would pass muster."

"I'm pretty sure that is what my state would do, we kind of are already," Michael of Connecticut, "and almost nobody would as you say, pass muster. It would be close to a state –wide ban."

"Not in Montana," Jack Robinson guessed. "I wouldn't be surprised if our guys got right into it. Maybe even had local militias in some towns, with meetings and drills."

Joyce added, "In fact, you already have militias don't you, Jack? We keep reading about bands of homophobic, anti-Semitic, and openly racist white supremacists and outcasts who call themselves militias, don't we?"

"Yeah," Michael added. "What about them?" More talk ensued.

Mary summed it up: "Under this plan it would be up to the states to deal with them; rein them in."

Harlan added, "Right, a state militia under the original 1792 configuration was well-regulated and the state, not the federal government, installed the chain of commands, the officers. The founders were adamant about this. States would have to regulate these modern groups today just as they did in the beginning."

They took another little break, and when they came back, Reverend Mansfield asked, "So, we're done at last?"

"Maybe," Jack Robinson. "There is one more thing." Everyone looked at him. "You've clipped the knees out from under the second amendment here – really set a precedent leading to the limitation and even confiscation at the state level of a whole class of firearms. How do we know that now that you've taken an inch, you won't come back and take a mile? How do we know you won't just go after some other gun? You've tried in the past, you know tried to outlaw hand guns. Remember the campaign to ban 'Saturday night specials'?" He added air quotes here.

Another long silence. Finally Mary of New York, answered. "I promise not to, Jack."

Everyone laughed. Jack would have no problems with Mary Kidd, but she caught their meaning and was ticked off. She flashed. "Look, my people die more than any others from hand guns, so if I can promise to leave them alone, that's saying something, isn't it."

Joyce agreed, "Sure it is Mary. And we here can all promise, too." Then it came to the whole crowd at once. "Let everybody in the country promise to abide by this compromise forever!"

They set right to work on a pledge. Joyce and Jack thought it would be called the Comprehensive Modern Militia Act pledge or the COMMA pledge. When they had finished, they were pleased. "We'll get as many people as we can to agree to take the pledge. Wouldn't it be wonderful if every American took this oath?" Doreen clapped her hands. This is what they came up with:

Modern Militia Pledge

I,_____a Citizen of the United States of America, resident of the State of _____, recognize that I am entitled to many rights and privileges of citizenship.

I also acknowledge and affirm that citizenship entails responsibilities and I hereby pledge to fulfill mine. I pledge, **whether armed or not** to:

- Uphold, protect, and defend the Constitution of the United States against all enemies, both foreign and domestic

- Obey the laws of our great country and my state

- Be prepared to securely keep and competently bear arms (2nd Amendment, Bill of Rights) if necessary for the protection of my person, my home, my state, and my country

- **If keeping and bearing arms**, to abide by the laws and regulations of the state in which my citizenship is recorded

- **If armed with a semiautomatic rifle** to register the same with my state's militia authorities and

- (1) Participate in such activities as may be required

-     (2) Abide by the directions of my militia's chain of command

-     (3)Advise authorities of both states should I move

-     (4) Maintain my weapon in my home state only and cross state lines only with authority of the governors of both the sending and the receiving states

-     **When carrying arms,** whether openly or concealed, always also carry proof of citizenship of my home state

-     **Report immediately and forcibly** to proper authorities all violations or anticipated violations of laws involving the use of firearms.

Signature _____

Name:

Date:

CC. Office of the Governor, State of Citizenship

They agreed they had done the best they could. None was optimistic that anything would change when they brought their plan back after the recess. Then Jack and Harlan both offered a final amendment. "You know, this pledge is open ended. Each citizen who pledges would be expected to honor the pledge forever, but when

42

it comes to implementation of our plan; don't you really think our bosses would have an easier time of it if this Comprehensive Modern Militia Act had a sunset provision like the last time they passed a limitation on semiautomatics?" They talked about that right though their last meal tonight; finally agreed to sunset COMMA in 20 years. Half of them wanted longer and half less time. They are laying out the outline of their agreement now.

Front Royal, VA 9:15 PM

They just finished their final drafts and Mansfield agreed to convey the plan on behalf of the team to each of the senators all with the greatest secrecy, of course. The Reverend is leaving right now. The others are staying one last night and will bug out in the morning right after breakfast. Can you believe it; I think they are taking up a collection for my college fund. They really are a nice group of people all smart, cool, and kind.

Johnny, are you sure about this? They keep worrying about secrecy. I don't know why. It seems like common sense to me. Both safety and the second amendment were addressed. What could be wrong with it? Anyhow, I'd hate to get them into trouble. Alice

Boston, MA 11:15 PM

Stick with them, Alice. There will be no trouble. Trust me. I'll follow up with this. You did really well kiddo. Let me know if there is anything new tomorrow.

Front Royal, VA 11:20 PM
OK, ILY. Alice

Front Royal, VA 10:07 AM

Morning Bro, They're gone. Reverend Mansfield did come in and join them for breakfast. He asked Joyce and Jack to summarize what they believed was good about the compromise they had worked out. Jack said, "We saved the 2nd Amendment; just as today, average citizens will be able to keep and bear arms."

Joyce said, "We finally have someone who can be held responsible in addition to the individual for the misuse of the semi automatic rifles."

"And finally we have reciprocity," Harlan added. "If I obey the laws of my state regarding my guns I can take them with me anywhere in the country."

"Except the semi's," Mary added.

"Of course," Doreen agreed.

"I think it is progress to have all permanent gun transfers be contingent on passing the background checks." Mary.

"There is a mechanism for removing semiautomatic rifles from the hands of people who lack the stability to have them." Joyce.

"I think your plan covers it all. It is comprehensive."

The Reverend Mansfield added. "And committing to two decades should give the country time to adapt to the new reality. Presumably the Congress will commission one or more studies to assess the effectiveness of the new law over time. It would be silly not to."

Jack added, "I think it is good that we have once again, you know, through the pledge, affirmed that gun ownership and patriotism are linked. We probably will never see a complete restoration of the Minute Man mentality, but it is a step in the right direction."

Then Mansfield said, "Tell me what is bad about it."

Harlan popped up; "The damned slippery slope. We will have to be super vigilant to make sure you don't come after every other gun, too."

"Come on, Harlan, relax. We all promised not to, and with luck a lot of others in the country will, too." Mary again. "I still feel it doesn't go far enough. In my heart it is unconscionable to allow all these military style weapons to remain in civilian hands. They simply are neither appropriate nor needed, but we came here to find a compromise and we did, I guess."

Doreen Dodge of Vermont added, "We did. It is just like the Yankee farmers who negotiated a horse trade. They both left feeling they had been robbed; one felt he had paid too much for the horse and other believed he had been paid too little. In Vermont they say that is how you know it was a good compromise – everyone is dissatisfied."

Laughter again. The Reverend Mansfield closed the breakfast with a brief speech. He praised them again. Told them that Reinhold Neibuhr had observed that the larger a group, the more selfish it is and the less likely it is to compromise for the greater good. "The six of you are a small group and you did it, not easily, but you succeeded. Unfortunately, it will be much harder for political parties with millions of members each to compromise. We can only hope, yes? But for now, please let me indulge." He even summoned me, Johnny, from the pantry. They all wanted me to be there, too. It was so sweet. Anyway, the Reverend quoted the King James Bible verse, Matthew 5:9, I believe. "Blessed are the peace makers for they shall be called the children of God."

He prayed for us all, too. Calling us peacemakers and Children of God. "May you all go in peace." I can tell you, the goodbyes after that were pretty tearful. I know I cried, brother. I'm going to miss them all.

We're cleaning up now. Housekeeping is already changing the beds. See you soon,
ILY Alice.

Epilogue
Boston, Massachusetts
July 4, 2018

The outcomes of the Greystone Surveillance were varied. I reached out to all of the participants in the planning retreat, to each of the six senators, and to the Reverend Doctor Robert Mansfield. Everyone was highly annoyed that I had so much information, and not one would add a comment, but the Reverend and two of the staff aides acknowledged at least that the retreat had occurred and that they had participated. It was enough. The editor approved the article I wrote and it was published on April 5th just as the Senate was returning from its recess. As you might guess, controversy ensued.

Not one of the Senators embraced the plan right away. Some were holding back to see which way the wind might blow, and others were outright hostile. The Defenders of the Second Admendment (DSA) and the Stop All Gun Violence Association (SAGVA), as predicted, denounced the aides' plan in the strongest terms. Soon, their principal senators followed suit. By late May, each of the participants in the Greystone retreat had received at least one death threat, and the FBI was involved. Oddly, Alice and I were not held accountable, one instance in which the messengers were not shot.

But it certainly looked like the compromise was dead on arrival, and for a time all of Doreen Dodge's Vermont farmers were convinced the compromise was a bad deal. It was roundly condemned from both sides. But then, a surprising thing happened. First a few: educators, clergy, then a few more, police rank and file members, and some academics began to speak up in favor of the Greystone Compromise. Soon, many more did also, and there emerged a movement.

An unknown donor or foundation appeared out of the woodwork and funded a small coordinating staff in DC independent of the DSA and the SAGVA groups. Almost at once, speakers and paraphernalia were at large across the land and COMMA pins and flags were soon in evidence everywhere. On lapel pins, handkerchiefs, and hoodies, they used the Flag of 1793 when the Militia Act first took effect.

By then Vermont and Kentucky had joined the original thirteen states, so for a while they tried having fifteen stars and fifteen stripes. It became quite recognizable. "I am a proud Modern American Militia Man" could be heard shouted in all sorts of places from the far right to the far left of the American spectrum; the former because the flag represented defense of the second amendment and the latter because it represented regulation of semiautomatic rifles.

As of this date, it is too soon to tell what will happen, but one thing is sure, this genie cannot be put back in the bottle. The Comprehensive Modern Militia Act may or may not be passed in the next Congress, but it is getting an airing in the bright light of day.

I had something to do with that I am sure. Had Alice not been where she was-a great bit of luck-the work of the aides would likely have been for naught; their bosses would have suppressed their reforms just as they rejected all others. So, some good may come of it next term. We shall see.

Meanwhile, Alice was fired straightaway, of course, just as soon as her role became known. She had broken no laws, and when my paper leaned in to make her case, the Greystone Lodge beat a hasty retreat from any further punitive actions. We found her a better job to finish up her gap year; she's an intern with the *Globe* here in Boston. The Greystone aides did take up a collection, a small one to be sure, but nonetheless it will help her pay college expenses next fall. And best of all, Alice has decided to start McDougal's program at Boston University. Journalism gets into your blood.

I believe it is still the case that Jack and Mary were bridging a pretty long gap in backgrounds proving that a Hawk from Montana and pacifist from Manhattan can successfully share the rent - at least in the District of Columbia. They are regularly proving that compromise can be a good thing.

I am going to throw modesty to the wind here and crow a little. The Greystone Surveillance won an award! Not a Pulitzer of course, but a local one here in Boston: The O'Brien for journalistic excellence. When they handed it over to me at the awards ceremony in the huge Park Plaza ball room everyone was there, but you know what the best thing was? It was knowing that efforts are under way to make it less likely that some nut with a semiautomatic rifle will come bursting through the doors and opening fire.

Meanwhile, this man's career is off to one sweet start.

Johnny Ames, Reporter
The Boston Globe

Acknowledgements:

None of the characters in this story ever lived. There is no Greystone Lodge. It is all fiction and any similarity to anything or anyone real is purely coincidental.

I am blessed with a broad array of friends and family members. I am sure that collectively, they encompass the entire spectrum of thought on the topic of guns. I am indebted to them for their insights. Some of them vehemently object to the suggested Greystone Compromise; claiming it goes too far. Others equally vehemently object saying it doesn't go far enough. The majority, I think, fall somewhere in between. In any case, they are not to blame for these ideas. I am.

One thing all of my family and friends do agree upon is this: In a functioning democracy, we absolutely most agree that it is the content of ideas, not their sources that matter. Ideas are like gems; at our best we assess their worth, both facets and flaws, objectively. It matters not from whence which quarry they came. They just are. So it is with the Greystone Compromise. Please evaluate, and respectfully discuss these ideas

Sincerely,

Publius
March 22, 2018

References:

Joseph Ellis, *The Quartet: Orchestrating the Second American Revolution, 1783 – 1789*. New York, Penguin Random House, 2015

Stephen P. Halbrook, *The Founders' Second Amendment: Origins of the Right to Bear Arms*. Chicago Ill, The Independent Institute, 2008

www.ingramcontent.com/pod-product-compliance
Lightning Source LLC
Chambersburg PA
CBHW032122280326
41933CB00009B/948